ESTONIA TRAVEl

Discover Estonia: a Journey through History, Nature, and Baltic, A complete guide for first timers

By

John Emmanuel

Table of contents

Welcome

Enter the enchanting country of Estonia, a gem in the northeastern part of Europe. Prepare to be captivated by this stunning Baltic nation's charm and allure as you begin your journey.

You'll be greeted by a mix of ancient history and modern innovation upon arrival. With medieval castles, picturesque towns, and cobblestone streets that invite you to discover their secrets, Estonia proudly displays its rich cultural heritage. Tallinn, the charming capital, will ship you back in time with its impeccably protected Old Town, an UNESCO World Legacy site. You'll be surrounded by towering spires, bustling markets, and a lively atmosphere that echoes the sounds of bygone eras as you take in the medieval atmosphere.

However, Estonia is not simply a time-capsule. Because of its cutting-edge digital advancements, it has been dubbed "e-Estonia," a thriving center of technology and innovation. In a nation where e-residency, digital government services, and online voting are the norm, you can firsthand experience the future. Estonia's obligation to innovation and business has made a powerful biological system, encouraging a lively startup culture and drawing in ability from around the globe.

Estonia's unspoiled landscapes, which include tranquil lakes, dense forests, and picturesque coastlines, are a haven for nature lovers. Explore the nation's numerous national parks, such as Lahemaa and Soomaa, which feature unspoiled wilderness and a wide variety of wildlife, while taking a moment to take in the crisp, clean air. With their rugged coastlines, idyllic beaches, and charming rural villages, the tranquil islands, including Saaremaa and Hiiumaa, provide a haven of peace.

The welcoming people of Estonia will share their stories and customs with you when you arrive. Enjoy traditional dishes like black bread, hearty soups, and mouthwatering smoked fish from Estonian cuisine. Also, don't forget to try the local favorite, Vana Tallinn, a sweet and smoky liqueur that reflects the country's spirit.

Welcome to Estonia, then! This tiny nation promises an unforgettable experience, whether you're there to learn about history, marvel at technological marvels, explore pristine nature, or simply enjoy the warm hospitality. Prepare to make priceless memories and discover the numerous wonders of Estonia.

Introduction

Hello, and welcome to Estonia, a charming gem in Northern Europe. Estonia is a nation that seamlessly combines tradition and innovation, and it is well-known for its fascinating history, breathtaking landscapes, and technological advancements. This tiny but vibrant nation, which is on the eastern shore of the Baltic Sea, has charmed tourists with its picturesque cities, ancient castles, and unwavering spirit of resilience.

The "Digital Republic" of Estonia has established itself as a global leader in digital innovation and technology. It was the birthplace of many groundbreaking initiatives, such as e-residency, which lets people from anywhere in the world set up and run a business online within the borders of the country. Estonia has developed a reputation for its cutting-edge digital infrastructure, which provides seamless internet connectivity and a thriving startup ecosystem to a population that embraces the digital world.

Estonia is known for its stunning natural beauty in addition to its technological achievements. From the captivating backwoods of Lahemaa Public Park to the pure sea shores of Pärnu and the beautiful islands dissipated along its coast, Estonia offers an abundance of outside encounters. During the winter, its diverse landscapes can be explored, ancient forests can be hiked through, and the mesmerizing dance of the Northern Lights can be seen.

The history of Estonia is a fascinating mosaic of influences. The country has been shaped by various nations, including the Danes, Swedes, Germans, and Russians, over the centuries. The unique cultural identity of Estonia is a fusion of the influences of each era. The country's capital, Tallinn, is home to an Old Town that has been designated as a UNESCO World Heritage Site. Here, Gothic spires, cobblestone streets, and medieval walls blend seamlessly with contemporary cafes, shops, and galleries.

Traditional song and dance festivals, the celebration of ancient pagan traditions, and a deep reverence for nature are all ways in which Estonians show their pride in their heritage. The preservation of centuries-old traditions and customs, such as sauna culture and a love for the Estonian national epic "Kalevipoeg," exemplify the nation's strong connection to its roots.

Estonia promises a one-of-a-kind and unforgettable experience whether you're looking for a glimpse into Estonia's long history, outdoor adventures in pristine natural landscapes, or the cutting-edge innovations of the digital age. Therefore, come and revel in the charm of this Baltic treasure and discover the buried treasures that await in Estonia.

Reasons why you should love Estonia

Estonia is adored for many reasons! The following are some compelling characteristics that make Estonia an intriguing and likable nation:

Technology Development: Estonia's advanced digital infrastructure and e-governance systems are well-known. It was the first nation to offer e-residency, which made it possible for people all over the world to start and run businesses online. The innovative mindset of Estonians is reflected in a variety of everyday activities and practices.

Pioneers of the web: Estonia is frequently alluded to as the "Baltic Silicon Valley" because of its flourishing tech startup biological system. It is responsible for the birth of Skype, TransferWise (now Wise), Bolt, and numerous other internationally renowned businesses. A thriving technology scene is the result of the country's entrepreneurial spirit and supportive environment.

Shocking Nature: Estonia's stunning scenery includes unspoiled forests, numerous lakes, and picturesque coastline. Forests cover nearly half of the country, making it an ideal destination for nature lovers. Estonia's diverse and captivating natural beauty ranges from Lahemaa National Park to the singular bogs of Soomaa.

Cultural and historical riches: Estonia has a rich history and culture despite its small size. Over the centuries, the country has been influenced by a variety of civilizations, resulting in a fascinating mix of Germanic, Russian, and Nordic influences. In Tallinn's Old Town, you can take in the medieval architecture or visit ancient castles and manor houses that give you a glimpse into Estonia's past.

Spa Culture and Saunas: In Estonian culture and everyday life, saunas hold a special place. The country has a long history of using saunas for socializing and relaxation. The Estonians enjoy spending time in saunas before taking a cool dip in a lake or the Baltic Sea nearby. Additionally, Estonia is well-known for its excellent spa facilities, which provide energizing experiences.

Festivals of music: Estonia is a heaven for music sweethearts, facilitating various top notch live events over time. The country's vibrant music scene is showcased by the well-known Tallinn Music Week, Parnu Film and Music Festival, and Viljandi Folk Music Festival, which draw artists from all over the world.

Sustainable and Clean Living: Estonia places a high value on environmental consciousness and sustainability. The country has made significant progress in implementing eco-friendly practices, such as focusing on recycling and waste management, making extensive use of renewable energy sources, and maintaining the public transportation system.

Inviting and Well disposed Individuals: The Estonian people are renowned for their welcoming nature, strong sense of community, and warmth. Even though they are reserved at first, once you get to know them, they are friendly and welcoming. The country's small size also contributes to its close-knit society, where connections and support from one another are valued.

Fun Things to Do in the Winter: The winter season in Estonia is magical and full of exciting activities. There are numerous ways to enjoy the snowy landscapes, including ice fishing, snowshoeing, and ice skating. You won't want to miss the beautiful winter wonderland in Estonia.

Unusual Language and Culture: Estonian is an extraordinary Finno-Ugric language, inconsequential to most other European dialects. It can be enjoyable to learn a few Estonian phrases. The summer solstice celebration (Jaanihtu) and the national song and dance festival (Laulupidu), which highlight the cultural pride and identity of the Estonian people, are also captivating traditions.

These are only a couple of justifications for why Estonia is a country worth cherishing. Its mix of innovation, nature, history, and culture makes a genuinely unmistakable and dazzling experience for occupants and guests the same.

Facts about Estonia

Some interesting facts about Estonia are as follows:

Location: The country of Estonia is in Northern Europe. It is separated from Finland by Latvia to the south, Russia to the east, and the Gulf of Finland to the north.

The largest and capital city: Tallinn, Estonia's largest city and capital, is also the country's capital. Tallinn is known for its very much protected middle age Old Town, which is an UNESCO World Legacy site.

Language: The authority language of Estonia is Estonian, which is a Finno-Ugric language firmly connected with Finnish. However, English is widely spoken, particularly among younger people and in urban areas.

Independence: Estonia declared independence from Russia in 1918, but the Soviet Union occupied the country during World War II and ruled it until 1991. After that, it became a democracy.

E-government: Estonia is known for its high level computerized foundation and e-taxpayer driven organizations. It was one of the first nations to allow non-residents to start and run businesses online with e-residency.

Connection to the internet: Estonia has one of the highest rates of internet use worldwide. Skype, a well-known voice and video calling application created by Estonian software engineers, was born there.

Education: Education is very important in Estonia. It has one of the highest literacy rates in the world, and its educational system is highly regarded worldwide, particularly in the STEM fields.

Wildlife and nature: In spite of being a little country, Estonia is known for its different normal scenes, including timberlands, wetlands, and north of 1,500 islands along its shore. It is home to numerous bird and animal species in addition to brown bears, lynxes, and wolves.

Revolution in Singing: The Singing Revolution was a peaceful movement for independence in Estonia at the end of the 1980s. Singing was a big part of the protest against Soviet rule that led to Estonia regaining its independence in 1991.

Saunas: In Estonian culture, saunas hold special significance. They are frequently utilized for unwinding, socializing, and health improvement and are thought to be an essential component of social life. Numerous Estonians have saunas in their homes or summer houses.

These facts reveal Estonia's fascinating past, technological advancements, and stunning natural beauty.

Estonia's Foreign Influence

Like many other nations, Estonia has been influenced in various ways by foreign influence. A country's political, economic, social, or cultural landscape is shaped or manipulated by external actors in order to advance their own interests. This is known as "foreign influence." The following are some significant aspects of Estonia's encounter with foreign influence:

Contextual History: Estonia has a long and complicated history marked by dominance and influence from abroad. Over time, the nation has been subject to various abilities, including Sweden, Russia, and Germany, which have left their engravings on Estonian culture and culture.

Soviet Union: When Estonia was compelled to join the Soviet Union, it experienced one of the most significant periods of foreign influence in its recent history. Estonian national identity was suppressed and Russification was promoted as a result of the Soviet government's imposition of its political ideology, economic system, and social structures on the country.

Independence after the Soviet Union: After the Soviet Union broke up in 1991, Estonia regained its independence. However, there were difficulties in constructing a democratic nation and its institutions, including attempts at external influence. Russia, which sought to maintain its sphere of influence and control over former Soviet territories, was one of these influences.

Influence from Russia: Due to its close proximity to Russia and large population of Russian-speaking people, Estonia has been particularly susceptible to Russian influence. Estonia has been the target of propaganda campaigns and state-controlled Russian media that spread inaccurate information and narratives that undermine Estonia's sovereignty and independence.

Cyber threats: In 2007, Estonia was the target of a significant cyberattack that was widely believed to have been launched by Russia. The attack disrupted services and caused widespread chaos by targeting media outlets, critical infrastructure, and government institutions in Estonia. This episode featured the weakness of nations to digital fighting and the potential for unfamiliar entertainers to take advantage of innovative shortcomings.

Membership in NATO and the European Union: Some safeguards against foreign influence have been provided by Estonia's integration into

NATO and the European Union (EU). Estonia's security has been improved as a result of its membership in these organizations, which have provided platforms for cooperation with other member states to address common challenges like cyber threats and disinformation campaigns. Countering Unfamiliar Impact: Estonia has taken a number of steps to protect its national security and counter foreign influence. Cybersecurity measures are being increased, media literacy is being promoted, and public awareness of propaganda and disinformation is being raised. In addition, Estonia has collaborated with partners around the world to share best practices and coordinate responses to influence campaigns from abroad.

It's critical to take note that unfamiliar impact is a complex and developing peculiarity, and its indications can change after some time. Estonia, as different nations, keeps on adjusting its methodologies to address new difficulties and safeguard its popularity based cycles and public interests despite unfamiliar impact.

Chapter One

Best Time to Visit Estonia

The best time to visit Estonia depends largely on your preferences and the activities you intend to participate in. There are various seasons in Estonia, each with its own set of experiences. The following is a breakdown of the various seasons and their characteristics to assist you in choosing the ideal time to visit:

Summer (June to August): The best time to visit Estonia is during the summer, when outdoor activities and the country's vibrant cultural events are at their best. Temperatures range from 15°C to 25°C (59°F to 77°F) and are generally pleasant. You can take in the medieval old towns, unwind on the gorgeous Baltic Sea beaches, and attend a variety of music festivals and outdoor concerts.

Spring (April to May) and Pre-winter (September to October): Compared to summer, these shoulder seasons have milder weather and fewer people. Spring is a wonderful time for nature lovers because it brings blooming flowers and green landscapes. Autumn is known for its vibrant foliage, which makes for beautiful landscapes. These seasons have temperatures ranging from 41°F to 59°F, or 5°C to 15°C. Without the summer crowds, this is the ideal time to explore national parks, hike, and enjoy cultural attractions.

Winter: November through February In the winter, temperatures in Estonia frequently dip below freezing. This is the ideal time to visit if you enjoy winter activities like ice skating, cross-country skiing, or going to Christmas markets. The charming old towns of the country have beautiful decorations, and you can see the magic of Estonia when it's covered in snow. Additionally, you might get a chance to see the magnificent Northern Lights.

It's important to remember that the weather can be hard to predict, so check the forecast before you go. Likewise, remember that sunlight hours are fundamentally more limited in winter contrasted with summer, which might affect your touring plans.

In the end, the best time to visit Estonia depends on your interests and the things you want to see and do. Choose a time of year that satisfies your preferences for the activities you enjoy the most.

Getting To Estonia

To go to Estonia, you have at least a couple choices relying upon your beginning area. Here is a general manual for assist you with getting to Estonia:

By Air:

The simplest and quickest method for arriving at Estonia from abroad is via air. Tallinn Airport (TLL), Estonia's international airport, is well-connected to major European and international cities. You can use a variety of travel websites to search for flights to Tallinn

Airport from your international airport of choice or directly through the websites of the airlines themselves. Regular flights to Tallinn are provided by a number of major airlines, including national carrier Nordica, Ryanair, Lufthansa, Air Baltic, Finnair, and others.

By boat:

You might want to think about taking a ferry to Estonia if you are coming from nearby countries like Finland or Sweden. Tallinn has a few ship terminals that get normal ship administrations from Helsinki, Finland, and Stockholm, Sweden. Tallink, Viking Line, and Eckerö Line are the most well-known ferry companies. The ship excursion can shift in term contingent upon the course, however it ordinarily requires around 2-3 hours from Helsinki and 15-18 hours from Stockholm.

By Bus:

You can also take a bus trip to Estonia if you are already in Europe. From neighboring nations, a number of international bus companies provide services to Estonia. Some of the major bus companies that provide routes to Tallinn from various European cities are Ecolines, Lux Express, and Eurolines. Keep in mind that bus travel may take longer than flying, but it may be less expensive.

On Trains:

Although many European countries do not have direct train connections, it is possible to travel to Estonia by train through its neighbors. For instance, you can take a train to the Estonian line city of Valga from Riga, Latvia, and afterward proceed with the excursion to Tallinn by transport or taxi. Checking train schedules and routes with national rail operators or international rail booking platforms is highly recommended.

Check the current travel restrictions and requirements, such as visa requirements, COVID-19 protocols, and any specific entry requirements set by the Estonian government, before traveling to the country. Before you go, make sure you have a valid passport and any necessary permits or visas.

To make your stay in Estonia more convenient, you should also think about making a reservation for a place to stay in advance and becoming familiar with the various forms of local transportation. Check the weather forecast for your travel dates and pack appropriate clothing for the season.

Have a wonderful time in Estonia!

Getting Around Estonia

You can use a variety of modes of transportation to get around Estonia. The nation's most widely used modes of transportation are as follows:

Transport Options:

Estonia has a proficient public transportation framework, particularly in bigger urban communities like Tallinn. You can get around Tallinn on buses, trams, and trolleybuses. Other cities and towns also offer public transportation, though the frequency of services varies. You can buy tickets from the driver or utilize a contactless card like the Tallinn Card for limitless travel inside a specific period.

Taxis:

In Estonia, taxis are readily available and a convenient mode of transportation, particularly for shorter distances within cities. You can find taxis at assigned taxi stands or flag down one in the city. In bigger urban communities, you can likewise utilize ride-hailing applications, for example, Bolt or Uber to book a taxi.

Rental Car:

Leasing a vehicle gives you the opportunity to investigate Estonia at your own speed, particularly in the event that you intend to visit more modest towns or country regions. Estonia has a lot of big car rental companies, and airports and city centers both have rental car services. Make sure you have a valid driver's license and are familiar with the local traffic laws.

Cycling:

Estonia is known for its advanced cycling foundation, making it a brilliant country for bicycle lovers. You can rent bicycles from a variety of bike-sharing services in cities like Tallinn and Tartu, and many cities have dedicated bike lanes. Cycling is a wonderful way to see the beautiful countryside and coast.

Boats and ferries:

Estonia has islands worth visiting, including Saaremaa and Hiiumaa, along its Baltic Sea coastline. Ships work routinely between the central area and these islands, giving an interesting travel insight. Boat excursions on lakes and rivers are another option for both leisure and transportation.

Domestic flights:

Domestic flights are an option if you want to get to more remote areas quickly or cover longer distances within Estonia. Flights interface significant urban communities and islands, giving a helpful and efficient choice. There are airports in the cities of Tartu, Pärnu, and Kuressaare that offer domestic flights.

It's important that Estonia has a minimized size, making it generally simple to go between urban communities. Also, the country has a good internet connection, so using digital maps or apps for navigation can help you get around.

Where To Stay in Estonia

Estonia is a beautiful country in Northern Europe that has beautiful landscapes, lively cities, and a lot to offer in terms of culture. There are a number of choices for where to stay in Estonia based on your preferences and interests. The following are some suggestions:

Tallinn: As the capital city of Estonia, Tallinn is a well known decision for guests. With its medieval charm, cobblestone streets, and well-preserved architecture, the Old Town of Tallinn, a UNESCO World Heritage Site, is a must-see. You can track down a scope of facilities, from lavish lodgings to spending plan well disposed lodgings, in and around the downtown area.

Tartu: Tartu is a university town and a center for culture and innovation.It has a lively atmosphere, a historic city center, and a pulsating scene at night. There are a variety of places to stay in Tartu, including guesthouses, apartments, and boutique hotels.

Pärnu: In the event that you're searching for a beachside escape, Pärnu is a famous hotel town situated on Estonia's west coast. It has beautiful parks, long sandy beaches, and a laid-back atmosphere. Pärnu offers a scope of lodgings, spa resorts, and guesthouses, a significant number of which are found near the ocean side.

Saaremaa: Consider staying on Saaremaa, Estonia's largest island, for a more natural and rural experience. It is well-known for its windmills, medieval castles, and unspoiled landscapes. You can stay in Kuressaare, the main town, or in rural guesthouses and cottages scattered throughout the island.

Viljandi: Viljandi is a small town that is well-known for its folk music scene and rich cultural heritage. It is tucked away among picturesque lakes and rolling hills. It is the location of the Viljandi Folk Music Festival, which draws musicians and tourists from all over the world. In Viljandi, you can track down comfortable guesthouses, lodgings, and occasion lofts.

National Park Lahemaa: Staying close to Lahemaa National Park gives nature lovers a chance to see Estonia's stunning natural landscapes. Manor houses, pristine forests, picturesque coastal areas, and hiking trails are all available in the park. Hotels, guesthouses, and camping sites can be found in nearby cities such as Rakvere and Käsmu.

Estonia has a lot more to offer than these few suggestions. Consider your inclinations, the exercises you need to take part in, and the climate you favor while picking where to remain in Estonia. Whether you're searching for authentic appeal, waterfront unwinding, or regular magnificence, Estonia has something to suit each voyager.

Accomodations in Estonia

Estonia, a stunning nation in Northern Europe, has numerous lodging options to suit a variety of preferences and budgets. There are a lot of places to stay, whether you're going to Tallinn, the vibrant capital city, or going to the charming countryside. Some popular choices are as follows:

Hotels: Estonia has a lot of hotels, from expensive establishments to ones that are affordable. Within the medieval Old Town of Tallinn, you'll find boutique hotels, internationally renowned chains, and historic accommodations. In addition to Tallinn, major cities like Tartu and Pärnu provide convenient lodging options.

Bed and breakfasts and guesthouses: Consider staying at a bed and breakfast or a guesthouse for a more intimate experience. These foundations are much of the time family-run and give a comfortable environment, customized administration, and an opportunity to cooperate with local people. Guesthouses are especially normal in rustic regions, offering a special look into Estonian field life.

Cottages and Vacation Villages: The natural landscapes of Estonia are ideal for outdoor enthusiasts. Holiday villages and cottages are popular places to stay for people looking for a peaceful getaway in the middle of nature. Saunas, barbecues, private lake access, and other amenities are frequently included in these accommodations.

Hostels: Hostels are a great option if you're on a budget and prefer a social atmosphere. Estonia has many hostels for backpackers and solo travelers, especially in Tallinn. Inns offer shared quarters style rooms as well as confidential rooms, and they frequently give collective spaces to mingling.

Farmstays: Consider staying at a farmstay to get a taste of Estonian hospitality and rural life. You can stay in these accommodations on a farm, take part in farm activities, and eat meals made from local ingredients. For families and nature enthusiasts, farmstays are an excellent choice.

Wellness and spa resorts: Estonia is well-known for its wellness and spa culture. Wellness treatments, saunas, hot springs, and other amenities are available at a number of resorts across the nation. These hotels are ideal for a reviving escape.

In order to make the most of your time in Estonia, it's best to book your lodging in advance, especially during peak tourist seasons. When making your decision, take into account things like the location, the amenities, and how close you are to places of interest or public transportation. Estonia's accommodations are certain to provide a comfortable and memorable experience, regardless of whether you choose a contemporary hotel in Tallinn or a cozy cottage in the countryside.

Things To Pack For Estonia Visit

Things you might want to pack for your trip to Estonia include the following:
Clothing:
Contingent upon the season, pack a blend of warm and cool dress. Layers should always be used.

shoes that are easy to walk in for city and nature trails.

Because the weather in Estonia can be unpredictable, wear a raincoat or umbrella.

Documents for Travel:

Legitimate identification (check its termination date to guarantee it's substantial however long your excursion might last).

Documents for travel insurance.

Tickets for the train, flight, or any other relevant mode of transportation.

Convenience reservations and contact data.

if you want to rent a car, get a driving license from another country.

Equipment and Accessories for Electronics:

chargers and power adapters for your electronic gadgets.

phone and any necessary accessories

Use a smartphone or camera to capture precious moments.

Portable power bank for portable charging.

Items for Personal Care and Medication:

Prescription drugs in their original containers and prescription copies.

Band-aids, painkillers, and any personal medications in a basic first aid kit.

items for personal hygiene (such as a toothbrush, toothpaste, or shampoo)

Use insect repellent and sunscreen, especially if you plan to visit during the summer.

Banking and money:

Euros or a travel card for cashless transactions in Estonian currency.

Credit and debit cards, and you should tell your bank about your plans to travel.

A limited quantity of money for crises or places that don't acknowledge cards.

Maps and Travel Guides:

a map of Estonia or a travel guidebook to help you get around and plan your itinerary.

a language translation app or phrasebook if you're not familiar with Russian or Estonian.

Miscellaneous:

a water bottle that can be reused to keep hydrated.

snacks for the trip or for taking on day trips.

umbrella or rain poncho in travel size.

Use a travel lock to keep your belongings safe.

Make sure you check the weather forecast and think about the specific activities you want to do in Estonia. This list should be used as a general guide, but you can change it to fit your needs and preferences. Have an amazing trip

Chapter Two

Estonia History

In Northern Europe, Estonia has a long and varied history that dates back thousands of years. An overview of Estonia's most important historical events and developments is as follows: The Old and Middle Ages:

The Stone Age: The Finno-Ugric tribes first settled the area that is now Estonia in the year 9000 BC. Fishing, hunting, and farming were the primary occupations of these tribes.

From the eighth to the eleventh hundreds of years, Estonia was much of the time visited and affected by Vikings, especially from Sweden and Denmark. During this time, trade routes and early political structures were established.

Rule by Denmark and Germany: Denmark and the German Livonian Brothers of the Sword took control of various parts of Estonia in the 12th century. The Teutonic Knights later assumed command and laid out the Parish of Riga.

Rule by Sweden and Russia:

The Swedish Age: Estonia came under Swedish control in the 16th century. During this time, Lutheranism spread and a centralized administration was established.

Great War in the North: The Great Northern War between Sweden and Russia at the beginning of the 18th century left Estonia devastated. Estonia was handed over to Russian rule thanks to the Treaty of Nystad in 1721.

Russian Independence and Empire:

Empire of Russia: Estonia was subjected to Russian policies of "russification," which included efforts to assimilate Russian culture and language. Industrialization and urbanization additionally occurred during this period.

Public Arousing: Estonia went through a national awakening at the end of the 19th century, with a growing sense of Estonian identity and aspirations for independence. Schools that taught Estonian as a second language, as well as literary and cultural organizations, were crucial.

Estonian Independence War: Estonia declared independence in February 1918, following the end of World War I and the Russian Revolution. The following war, the Estonian War of Independence, saw Estonia successfully defend its independence from both German and Russian forces.

During the Wartime: Estonia became a democratic republic during the interwar period. It achieved significant economic expansion, implemented land reforms, and established a progressive legal system.

The Soviet Union and its successors:

Soviet Control: In 1940, the Soviet Association involved Estonia under the Molotov-Ribbentrop Agreement. As a result, Estonians were expelled in large numbers and Soviet rule was established, which lasted until the early 1990s.

Revolution in Singing: In Estonia, a nonviolent mass movement known as the Singing Revolution began toward the end of the 1980s. After the Soviet Union collapsed in 1991,

Estonia regained its independence through peaceful protests, singing events, and the restoration of national symbols.

Estonia today: Estonia has transformed into a modern democracy since regaining independence. It has joined the European Association and NATO, carried out monetary changes, and embraced innovative progressions, becoming known as a computerized society.

Estonia is a modern nation with a thriving economy, a strong emphasis on education and innovation, and a diverse cultural heritage. It keeps its historical roots while evolving and shaping its future.

Geography and Climate of Estonia

Estonia is a country in Northern Europe that is bounded by the Baltic Sea to the west, Russia to the east, Latvia to the south, and the Gulf of

Finland to the north. It is well-known for its diverse geography and unique climate. Let's find out more about Estonia's climate and geography:

Geography:

Estonia has more than 2,000 islands in the Baltic Sea, the largest of which are Saaremaa and Hiiumaa. Its total land area is about 45,227 square kilometers, or 17,462 square miles. Suur Munamägi, located just 318 meters (1,043 feet) above sea level, is the nation's highest point. The terrain in the country is relatively flat.

Forests cover nearly half of Estonia's land area, and there are a lot of them. The Narva River, Lake Peipus, and Lake Vrtsjärv are just a few of its numerous lakes and rivers. Various sandy seashores and limestone bluffs portray the 3,794-kilometer (2,357-mile) shoreline.

Climate:

Estonia has a mild climate because it is close to the Baltic Sea and the North Atlantic Ocean. Winters are typically bitter, while summers are typically mild. The following are the main characteristics of the climate in Estonia:

Summers last from June to August. With normal temperatures going from 15 to 20 degrees Celsius (59 to 68 degrees Fahrenheit), summers in Estonia are somewhat gentle and cool. The inland areas typically feel a little bit warmer, while the sea breeze typically makes the coastal areas feel a little bit cooler.

Winter months: December through February In Estonia, winter temperatures frequently dip below freezing. The average temperature is between -5 and 0 degrees Celsius, or 23 and 32 degrees Fahrenheit. There is a lot of snow during this time, and the country's lakes and rivers frequently freeze.

Spring and autumn (September to November): Gentle temperatures and moving weather conditions portray the temporary times of spring and fall. The weather can be very unpredictable during these months, with occasional changes in temperature and precipitation.

Estonia experiences a fairly even distribution of precipitation throughout the year, with an average annual precipitation of between 24 and 31 inches and a range of 600 to 800 millimeters.

The coastal areas typically receive more precipitation than the inland regions.

In conclusion, Estonia's geography consists of flat plains, forests, lakes, and islands. Summers are cool and winters are cold in this mild climate. The country's diverse natural features will make it a fascinating destination for outdoor enthusiasts.

People and Culture of Estonia

Estonia is a beautiful country in Northern Europe that is known for its unique culture, resilient people, and extensive history. Throughout its history, the culture of Estonia has been shaped by a complex interaction of influences from various neighboring nations. Let's take a deeper look into the fascinating culture and people of Estonia.

The Past and Its Influences:

With influences from Baltic, Nordic, and Slavic cultures, Estonia has a long and varied history. Throughout the long term, the locale has been subject to different abilities, including the Danish, Swedish, and Russian domains. The distinctive cultural mix that is Estonia today is the result of these influences.

Language:

Estonian is a Finno-Ugric language that is similar to Finnish but not as much as Hungarian. Estonian is one of the most difficult languages for non-native speakers to learn, and its speakers take pride in their language. The majority of the population speaks Estonian fluently as a result of efforts to preserve and promote the language.

Nature and kindness:

Despite the fact that they may initially appear reserved, Estonians are renowned for their warm hospitality. Estonians are usually open, helpful, and friendly once you get to know them. The Estonian way of life has been influenced by the country's breathtaking natural beauty, which includes vast forests, crystal-clear lakes, and picturesque coastline. Activities like hiking, camping, and picking berries are popular pastimes for many Estonians.

Traditions and mythology:

Folklore and traditions are deeply ingrained in Estonian culture. The country's cultural heritage has been significantly protected thanks to folk songs, or "regilaul." Estonian culture also includes handicrafts, colorful folk costumes, and traditional dances. The ancient practice of taking a sauna bath is very important to Estonian culture because it is seen as a social activity that helps people relax and clean their bodies and minds.

Arts and Music:

Estonia is well-known for its choral singing tradition and vibrant music scene. Every five years, thousands of singers from all over the country gather in Tallinn for the Estonian Song Festival to perform both traditional and contemporary music. Additionally, Estonia has produced internationally acclaimed classical composers like Veljo Tormis and Arvo Pärt. With a thriving theater, dance, and visual arts scene, the nation embraces the arts.

New Ideas and Technology:

Estonia is now recognized as one of the world's most digitally advanced nations. The e-governance, e-residency, and secure digital identity systems that the Estonian government has implemented are just a few examples of digital initiatives. Estonia's leadership position in the technology sector has been bolstered by this focus on technology and innovation, which has also attracted digital nomads and entrepreneurs from all over the world.

Wellness and saunas:

Because they help people unwind and feel refreshed, saunas are an important part of Estonian culture. Many Estonians have their own personal saunas at home or in their summer cottages, as sauna practices are deeply ingrained. Saunas are regarded as places for mental and physical health, and they are frequently enjoyed with loved ones. After a session in the sauna, Estonians frequently take a cool dip in a nearby lake or the Baltic Sea.

Estonian culture and people are a beautiful combination of traditions, historical influences, and a forward-thinking mindset. While embracing modernity and innovation, Estonians are extremely proud of their heritage. An experience that reveals a profound appreciation for nature, art, and community is learning about Estonia's one-of-a-kind culture and making connections with its resilient people.

Art and Music of Estonia

The small Baltic nation of Estonia in Northern Europe has a rich cultural heritage that includes music and art. Throughout the long term, Estonian craftsmen and performers have made huge commitments to different creative developments and kinds. Let's delve deeper into Estonian music and art.

Estonian art:

Folk and traditional art: Folk art traditions are deeply ingrained in the rural history of Estonia. Crafts like embroidery, pottery, weaving, and woodwork have been handed down through the generations. Nature, animals, and folk tales are frequently depicted in traditional patterns and motifs. Festivals and cultural events celebrate the vibrant textiles and intricate designs.

Romanticism in America: The National Awakening was a time of cultural awakening in Estonia in the late 19th and early 20th centuries. An artistic movement that sought to define and celebrate national identity was embraced by artists. Landscapes and historical scenes that were influenced by Estonian folklore and history were created by artists like Johann Köler and Kristjan Raud.

Contemporary and Modern Art: There are a lot of galleries and museums dedicated to contemporary art in Estonia. The nation has created globally perceived specialists like Jüri Arrak, Leonhard Lapin, and Kaido Ole. Painting, sculpture, installation, video art, and performance art are all forms of contemporary Estonian art.

Estonian music:

Classical Music: Unique vocal styles distinguish Estonian traditional music. A humankind-recognized intangible cultural heritage is the polyphonic singing style called "regilaul." It includes various voices singing in equal fifths or fourths. Estonian folk music also includes the kannel, a traditional plucked string instrument.

Music for Chorus: Estonia is known as the "singing nation" due to its extensive choral heritage. The Estonian Song Festival, held every five years, is a huge celebration of choral music. Choirs are very important to Estonian society. International acclaim has been given to the Estonian National Male Choir and the renowned Estonian Philharmonic Chamber Choir.

Traditional Music: Arvo Pärt, who is regarded as one of the most significant living composers of classical music, is one of the notable composers that Estonia has produced. Pärt is well-known all over the world for his minimalist and spiritually influenced music. Erkki-Sven Tüür, Veljo Tormis, and Eduard Tubin are three other well-known Estonian composers.

Experimental and Contemporary Music: Additionally, Estonia's contemporary music scene is thriving. The Tallinn Music Week, a yearly live performance and industry meeting, grandstands a large number of classifications, including rock, pop, electronic, and exploratory music. Emerging Estonian and international artists can present themselves on stage at the festival.

Estonia's music and art scenes have flourished in recent years, incorporating contemporary and traditional elements. The country's rich social legacy proceeds to motivate and impact its specialists, guaranteeing that Estonia stays a dynamic center point of imaginative inventiveness.

Festivals in Estonia

Estonia, a tiny Baltic nation in Northern Europe, has a rich cultural heritage that is celebrated throughout the year through a variety of festivals and events. A one-of-a-kind experience for both locals and visitors alike, these festivals provide a glimpse into Estonian traditions, folklore, music, and the arts. The following are some notable Estonian festivals:

Festival of Songs (Laulupidu): Every five years, Tallinn, the capital of Estonia, plays host to a significant cultural event known as the Estonian Song Festival. Traditional choral music is performed by thousands of musicians, choirs, and singers from all over Estonia. The festival has a long and rich history and helped to build national identity during the Soviet era. UNESCO has designated it a Masterpiece of Humanity's Oral and Intangible Heritage.

Festival of Folk Music in Viljandi: Traditional folk music from Estonia and around the world is celebrated at this annual festival in Viljandi, a charming town. Attendees can fully immerse themselves in the vibrant folk culture at the festival's diverse lineup of performances, workshops, and dance parties. For fans of music, it's a must-attend event that combines contemporary and traditional sounds perfectly.

Parnu Film Festival, also known as Pärnu Filmifestival: The Parnu Film Festival, one of

Estonia's most important film festivals, presents a diverse selection of domestic and international films. Film enthusiasts, directors, producers, and actors gather to appreciate cinematic art at the event. The festival is a prominent platform for the Estonian film industry because it features screenings, workshops, panel discussions, and awards ceremonies.

Black Nights Film Festival (PFF) in Tallinn: The Tallinn Black Nights Film Festival, which takes place in the capital, is one of Northern Europe's most important and largest annual film festivals. It shows a wide range of international films, including documentaries, feature films, and short films. In addition, industry events, workshops, and discussions are held at the festival, which serves as a platform for upcoming filmmakers and encourages cultural exchange.

Music week in Tallinn: As a main live concert and gathering in the Baltics, Tallinn Music Week draws in craftsmen, music industry experts, and music sweethearts from around the world. A wide variety of musical styles are on display at the event, including rock, pop, electronic, and classical music. Tallinn Music Week offers seminars, networking opportunities, and workshops to help the music industry grow in addition to performances by both established and emerging artists.

Seto Kuningriigi Päevad's Kingdom Days: The unique Seto cultural heritage in Southeastern Estonia is celebrated on Seto Kingdom Days. Visitors can experience the distinctive customs of the Seto ethnic group by attending the festival, which features traditional Seto music, dance, crafts, and food. Cultural events like handicraft workshops, exhibitions, and guided tours of the picturesque Seto villages are part of Seto Kingdom Days.

These are just a few of the many different kinds of festivals that take place throughout the year in Estonia. For both locals and visitors, each festival provides an opportunity to learn about Estonian culture, traditions, and artistic expressions.

Chapter Three

10 Top Attractions in Estonia

Ten of Estonia's best attractions are as follows:

Old Town of Tallinn: Investigate the middle age appeal of Tallinn's Old Town, an UNESCO World Legacy Site. Meander through cobblestone roads, visit notable structures, and appreciate amazing perspectives from Toompea Slope.

National Park Lahemaa: The largest national park in Estonia, on the northern coast, has a lot to offer in terms of beauty. Explore its numerous landscapes, which include picturesque coastal areas, lakes, wetlands, and forests.

Tartu College: Estonia's oldest and most prestigious university, Tartu University, is well worth a visit. Take in the stunning architecture, such as the iconic main building of the university and the Botanical Gardens.

Strand Pärnu: Pärnu, the summer capital of Estonia, has pristine beaches where you can unwind. Along the picturesque Baltic Sea coastline, indulge in sunbathing, swimming, and a variety of water sports.

Island of Saaremaa: Take a trip to Estonia's largest island, Saaremaa. Experience the island's distinctive culture, the impressive Kuressaare Castle, and its unique natural environment.

Museum of Kumu Art: At the Kumu Art Museum in Tallinn, you can get a taste of Estonia's art scene. The Estonian art that is on display in the museum spans the past and the present.

National Park of Soomaa: Explore the "Land of Bogs," the wetlands of Soomaa National Park. You can take guided canoe trips, hike through pristine forests, and see the park's exceptional wildlife on a variety of excursions.

TV Tower in Tallinn: From the Tallinn TV Tower's observation deck, take in panoramic views of Tallinn. With the tower's one-of-a-kind "Walk on the Edge" attraction, you can feel the rush of walking on the edge.

Castle Haapsalu: In the coastal town of Haapsalu, pay a visit to the charming Haapsalu Castle. Attend concerts in the castle courtyard, take in the medieval architecture, and learn about the fascinating history of the castle.

Region of Setomaa: In the Setomaa region in southeastern Estonia, discover the Seto people's cultural heritage. Take in the distinctive Seto cuisine, take in vibrant handicrafts, and wander through traditional villages.

These sights give you a glimpse of Estonia's fascinating culture, natural beauty, and long history.

Outdoor Activities in Estonia

Estonia, a beautiful country in Northern Europe, has a lot to offer adventurers and nature lovers alike in terms of outdoor activities. Even though Estonia is a small country, it has many different landscapes, like forests, lakes, rivers, coastal areas, and even islands. This makes it a great place to go outside and explore. In Estonia, you can participate in the following popular outdoor activities:

Nature and hiking trails: Estonia's extensive network of hiking trails allows visitors to fully appreciate the country's breathtaking natural beauty. On the northern coast, the Lahemaa National Park has well-marked trails that take you through beautiful forests, coastal cliffs, and old manor houses. The "Land of Bogs," Soomaa National Park, offers unique hiking opportunities through wetlands and marshes. Additionally, scenic trails with stunning views of lakes and rolling hills can be found in the Otepää region in southern Estonia.

Cycling: With a well-developed network of cycling paths and routes, Estonia is a nation that welcomes bicycles. The country's level territory makes it appropriate for relaxed rides and longer cycling visits. The Baltic Coastal Hiking Route, which runs along the coast and gives cyclists beautiful views of the Baltic Sea, is a popular choice. With their tranquil roads and charming rural landscapes, the islands of Saaremaa and Hiiumaa also offer excellent cycling opportunities.

Kayaking and canoeing: Estonia is great for canoeing and kayaking enthusiasts because it has many rivers, lakes, and coastal areas. The tranquil waters and picturesque landscapes of the Ahja River in southeastern Estonia make it a peaceful place to paddle. With its flooded forests and meandering rivers, the Soomaa National Park is a favorite destination for kayakers because it is a unique way to see the natural wonders of the area.

Observing Wildlife: Estonia's different biological systems support a rich exhibit of untamed life, and nature devotees will track down sufficient chances for birdwatching and natural life spotting. During the spring and autumn months, thousands of birds flock to Matsalu National Park, a major hub for their migration. Eagles, cranes, swans, geese, and other species can all be seen here. Seal watching is another popular activity along Estonia's coast, particularly on the islands of Saaremaa and Hiiumaa.

Camping: Estonia's natural landscapes and abundance of forests make it a great place to camp. Numerous protected areas and national parks offer designated camping sites with basic amenities. Camping lets you fully immerse yourself in the natural environment of Estonia and take pleasure in the peace and quiet of the great outdoors.

Extreme sports: Estonia has a lot of adventure sports for people who want a rush of adrenaline. Rock climbers flock to Lahemaa National Park because of the impressive limestone cliffs and exciting challenges they present. The country's lakes and rivers are ideal for fishing and boating, and the country's coastal areas offer opportunities for windsurfing, kitesurfing, and sailing.

Getting Around the Islands: The stunning islands of Estonia are well-known for providing a one-of-a-kind outdoor experience. The most populous island, Saaremaa, is home to traditional windmills, medieval castles, and picturesque landscapes. Another popular island destination is Hiiumaa, which is famous for its unspoiled natural environment and lighthouses. Hiking, cycling, and discovering charming coastal villages are all great activities on these islands.

It is important to note that Estonia has different seasons, with the summer months being the most popular for outdoor activities due to the milder weather. However, each season has its own charm, and even in the winter, you can enjoy snowshoeing, ice skating, and cross-country skiing.

Nature Tour of Estonia

When it comes to nature tours, the tiny country of Estonia in Northern Europe is a hidden gem. Estonia is home to a wide variety of landscapes despite its small size, such as pristine forests, captivating wetlands, picturesque coastal areas, and tranquil lakes. A nature tour in Estonia is a one-of-a-kind chance to see the country's incredible natural beauty and its abundant flora and fauna.

The extensive forest cover in Estonia is one of the highlights of a nature tour. Forests cover nearly half of the country's land area and provide numerous plant and animal species with abundant habitat. The forests of Estonia are renowned for their tranquility, making them ideal for peaceful hikes and walks. Visitors can discover a variety of wildflowers, vibrant mosses, and towering trees as they explore the ancient woodland. Deer, foxes, boars, and a wide variety of bird species are just a few of the elusive animals that nature enthusiasts might come across.

The unique wetlands of Estonia, which include bogs and marshes, are preserved and protected as nature reserves. The abundance of plant species, including rare orchids and carnivorous plants, that can be found in these wetland areas makes them unique in terms of their rich biodiversity. Visitors can enjoy the ethereal beauty of the wetlands while learning about their ecological significance by walking along the wooden boardwalks that traverse them. The variety of waterfowl and migratory birds that make their homes in these wetland habitats will delight birdwatchers.

The stunning views of the Baltic Sea and its pristine beaches from Estonia's coast are just as captivating. Saaremaa and Hiiumaa, two of the country's western islands, are well-known for their rugged beauty, charming fishing towns, and distinctive flora and fauna. Visitors can view nesting seabirds while exploring the coastal cliffs and, with luck, spot seals basking in the sun on the rocky shores.

Additionally, Estonia is well-known for the numerous lakes that dot the country's landscape and offer opportunities for recreation and relaxation. The largest lake in the nation, Lake Peipus, is a haven for boaters and anglers. Fish abound in its tranquil waters, and the countryside that surrounds it offers picturesque views and idyllic picnic spots. Additionally, nature lovers flock to the picturesque Lake

Ülemiste, which is close to Tallinn, the capital, for a tranquil escape from the city.

Estonia has a vast network of national parks and nature reserves to make nature tours more enjoyable. The country's pristine ecosystems are showcased in these protected areas, which offer visitors numerous hiking, wildlife viewing, and nature photography opportunities. Lahemaa National Park, renowned for its diverse landscapes, and Soomaa National Park, renowned for its vast floodplain forests and yearly flooding phenomenon, are two notable national parks.

In conclusion, a nature tour in Estonia promises to be an immersive experience amid unspoiled natural beauty. Estonia has a wide variety of landscapes to explore, including picturesque coastlines, tranquil lakes, enchanting forests, and captivating wetlands. Estonia's nature tours are certain to leave you with lasting memories and a profound appreciation for the country's remarkable biodiversity, regardless of whether you are looking for tranquility, encounters with wildlife, or just a connection with nature.

Setting Budget

To ensure that your trip to Estonia is comfortable and enjoyable without costing you too much, it's wise to set a budget. A step-by-step guide to setting a budget for your trip is provided below:

Determine how long you will be there: Your overall budget will be significantly impacted by the length of your visit. How many days or weeks you intend to spend in Estonia should be decided.

Examine your options for lodging: Look for a variety of places to stay, such as guesthouses, vacation rentals, hotels, and hostels. Find the option that best suits your needs and budget by taking into account the location, amenities, and price of each option.

Cost estimates for transportation: Evaluate the available modes of transportation within Estonia. Research the costs of each mode of transportation and decide whether you will be traveling by car, plane, train, bus, or train. Also, think about how much it will cost to get around the country, like renting a car or taking public transportation.

Make a plan for your excursions and sights: Make a list of the places you want to visit and the tours, museums, and activities you want to do. Examine the prices of tickets, entrance fees, and any other costs associated with these activities. Choose the ones you're most interested in and can afford first.

Consider the cost of meals: Find out how much a meal out in Estonia costs on average. Determine whether you will eat at a cafe, restaurant, or self-catering location. Consider the number of meals you intend to eat out each day and the associated costs.

Make provision for a variety of expenses: Make sure to include unexpected costs like medical bills or travel insurance as well as additional costs like souvenirs, shopping, and snacks. It's always a good idea to have extra money set aside for unforeseen circumstances.

Determine your daily spending limits: Divide the total budget by the number of days you will be in Estonia once you have an estimate of your expenses. You will receive a daily limit for your spending that you can use as a guide to stay within your budget.

Look for opportunities to cut costs: Consider cost-saving measures like booking facilities ahead of time, utilizing public transportation rather than taxis, settling on free or minimal expense attractions, and investigating reasonable eating choices like nearby business sectors or road food slows down.

Keep tabs on your costs: Keep track of your spending during your trip to make sure you stay within your budget. Write down your expenses and compare them to your budget in a spreadsheet, budgeting app, or notebook.

Modify your spending plan as needed: Assuming you observe that you're surpassing your everyday spending limit in specific regions, search for ways of scaling back costs or redistribute assets from different regions of your financial plan. You will be able to get the most out of your resources if you are adaptable and flexible.

Keep in mind that these are only general guidelines; your spending limit will be determined by your travel preferences and preferences. You can enjoy your trip to Estonia while staying within your means if you plan ahead and monitor your spending.

Chapter Four

Visa Requirements

This is general information about Estonia's visa requirements. Please be aware, however, that visa policies can change over time, so official sources like the Estonian Ministry of Foreign Affairs or consular services should be used to confirm the most recent information. An overview of Estonia's visa requirements can be found here.

Unrestricted Entry: For a certain amount of time, visitors from certain nations do not need a visa to visit Estonia. The length of sans visa stay differs in view of the nation of citizenship. The United States, Canada, Australia, the United Kingdom, and the majority of member states of the European Union (EU) and Schengen Area are examples of countries that do not require visas.

Visa for Schengen: Since Estonia is a member of the Schengen Area, traveling between its member countries does not require a visa. You may need to apply for a Schengen Visa through the Estonian embassy or consulate in your home country if you are a citizen of a nation that does not require a visa. You can travel to Estonia and other Schengen nations with the Schengen Visa for a maximum of 90 days within a 180-day period.

How to Apply for a Visa: Typically, you need to fill out an application form, provide the necessary documentation, and pay the appropriate fees to apply for a visa. Depending on the type of visa you are applying for (for example, tourist, business, or study), the specific requirements may differ. A return ticket, a current passport-sized photo, a travel itinerary, proof of lodging, proof of financial means, and travel insurance are all common requirements.

Long haul Stay: On the off chance that you intend to remain in Estonia for over 90 days or participate in exercises, for example, work or study, you might have to apply for a public visa or a home license. For long-term stays, the requirements and application process are more complicated and may require additional documentation like a letter of acceptance from an educational institution or a job offer.

Further Requirements: It is essential to keep in mind that visa requirements can vary depending on your citizenship country, the purpose of your visit, and other factors. Visa requirements may be influenced by bilateral agreements between some nations and Estonia. In addition, COVID-19 travel restrictions and health precautions may be in place; consequently, it is essential to verify the most recent information prior to making plans for your trip.

I recommend visiting the Estonian Ministry of Foreign Affairs' official website or contacting the closest Estonian embassy or consulate in your country for up-to-date and accurate information about Estonia's visa requirements.

Entry Requirements

Consult official sources like government websites or the Estonian embassy or consulate in your country for the most up-to-date information because travel regulations can change frequently. The following are the fundamental requirements to enter Estonia:

Current Passport: Check to see that your passport still has at least six months left on it after the time you plan to spend in Estonia.

Requirements for a Visa: Determine whether you need a visa to enter Estonia. Your nationality and the purpose of your visit both influence the requirements for a visa. For short-term stays, citizens of member states of the European Union (EU) and the European Economic Area (EEA) are not required to have a visa.

Entry Restrictions for COVID-19: There may be additional entry requirements and restrictions imposed as a result of the ongoing COVID-19 pandemic. For the most recent information regarding COVID-19 entry requirements, including vaccination, testing, and quarantine measures, consult the official websites of the Estonian government or get in touch with the Estonian embassy or consulate that is closest to you.

Zone Schengen: Estonia is a part of the Schengen Area, which lets people move freely between its member countries without having to worry about checking their own borders. Check that you meet the requirements for entry into the Schengen Area if you intend to visit other Schengen nations in addition to Estonia.

Accommodation Documentation: Prepare any necessary proof of your stay, such as hotel reservations, an invitation letter from a host, or other relevant documentation, to demonstrate your accommodations in Estonia.

Obtainable Funds: Have enough money on hand to cover your expenses while you are in Estonia. This can be demonstrated with cash, credit cards, or bank statements.

Insurance for Travel: During your time in Estonia, it's a good idea to have travel insurance that covers medical bills and emergencies. Even though it might not be required by law, it is highly recommended.

Ticket to Return: To show that you intend to leave Estonia within the allotted time, you may be asked to provide evidence of a return or onward ticket in some cases.

Rules for Customs: To ensure that you comply with any restrictions or allowances on the items you are bringing into the country, familiarize yourself with Estonia's customs regulations.

Before making plans for your trip, be sure to check the official websites of the Estonian government or the Estonian embassy or consulate closest to you for the most up-to-date and accurate information on entry requirements.

General Safety Tips

When visiting or living in Estonia, the following general safety guidelines should be kept in mind:

Security for Oneself: Although Estonia is generally safe, you should proceed with caution as you would in any other location. To avoid theft or pickpocketing, be aware of your surroundings, especially in crowded areas, and keep an eye on your belongings.

Crisis Administrations: Make yourself aware of Estonia's emergency phone numbers. Police, fire, and medical emergencies can all be handled by dialing 112, the general emergency number.

Documents for Travel: Securely store your passport, identification, and other essential travel documents. Making copies of these documents and keeping them separate from the originals is a good practice. Having copies will make it easier to get replacements in the event of loss or theft.

Security in Transportation: Assuming you're utilizing public transportation, particularly transports and cable cars, be wary of your own things. To prevent theft, keep an eye on your pockets and bags. Lock your car when you travel by car and don't leave valuables inside.

Safety in Nature: Estonia is known for its stunning natural landscapes, which include forests and national parks. Be sure to stick to the marked trails and paths when exploring these areas. Be aware of the wildlife in the area, adhere to any safety instructions or warnings, and do not feed or disturb the animals.

Weather Warnings: Throughout the year, Estonia experiences a variety of weather conditions. Dress warmly and be ready for icy conditions in the winter. Stay hydrated and protect yourself from the sun during the summer, especially if you spend a lot of time outside.

Cybersecurity and the Internet: When using public Wi-Fi networks, use caution just like you would in any other country. On unsecure networks, you should avoid making financial transactions or gaining access to sensitive data. Utilize a virtual confidential organization (VPN) for added security.

Services for Health and Medicine: Ensure that you have appropriate health insurance that covers your Estonian medical expenses. The emergency number is 112, and you can call for help if you need it. Travel insurance that covers medical evacuation is strongly recommended, particularly if you intend to participate in adventure activities.

Observe Local Laws and Traditions: Learn as much as you can about Estonian customs and laws. To ensure a safe and smooth trip, honor local customs, rules, and regulations.

Consuming Water: In most cases, Estonian tap water is safe to drink. However, you can drink bottled water, which is widely available, if you are concerned.

Keep in mind that these are general safety advice, and it's always a good idea to research and stay up to date on specific safety rules for the Estonian region you want to visit.

Health Safety Consideration

In Estonia, health safety concerns encompass a variety of public health and well-being issues. Consider these important points:

Medical system: The healthcare system in Estonia is well-developed and provides universal access to healthcare services. The country has a network of hospitals, clinics, and primary care centers to guarantee adequate healthcare coverage, and the system is based on mandatory health insurance.

Response to COVID-19: Estonia, like many other nations, has focused on controlling the COVID-19 pandemic. To stop the virus from spreading, the government has taken steps like testing, tracking down contacts, and vaccination campaigns. It is essential to keep up with the most recent guidelines and adhere to authorities' suggestions regarding health.

Vaccinations: Vaccines against a variety of diseases are available through an active vaccination program in Estonia. Children receive routine vaccinations, and adults can get vaccines against influenza, tetanus, diphtheria, and other diseases that can be avoided. It is essential to adhere to vaccination schedules and seek advice from medical professionals regarding any particular vaccine requirements.

Food Security: In order to safeguard public health, Estonia places a premium on food safety regulations. Food production, processing, and distribution are monitored by the Estonian Veterinary and Food Board to ensure compliance with hygiene and safety regulations. Food safety concerns should be reported, proper labeling should be looked for, and cooking and storage instructions should be followed.

Security in the environment: Estonia works hard to keep the environment healthy and clean. Standards for safe drinking water are upheld, pollution levels are monitored and controlled, and sustainable practices are promoted. It is crucial to participate in environmentally responsible waste management and recycling practices as well as to support environmental initiatives.

Health and Safety at Work: To safeguard the health and safety of employees, Estonia has regulations in place. The provision of a safe working environment, the performance of risk assessments, and the implementation of preventative measures are all obligations on the part of employers. Employees ought to be aware of their rights and should notify the appropriate authorities of any safety concerns.

Services for Emergencies: There are fire departments and emergency medical services (EMS) in Estonia's well-developed emergency response system. For immediate assistance in an emergency, dial the emergency number "112." In order to provide immediate assistance when it is required, it is essential to have a fundamental understanding of CPR and first aid techniques.

Mental Health Assistance: A person's overall well-being is largely impacted by their mental health. Counseling, therapy, and psychiatric care are just a few of the mental health services available in Estonia. Reaching out to healthcare professionals or helplines can provide support and direction if you or someone you know is struggling with mental health issues.

Keep in mind that safety and health concerns may change over time. To safeguard your own health and the health of others, it's best to stay up to date on the most recent guidelines, consult reputable sources like the Estonian Health Board, and take the necessary precautions.

Estonia Currency

The Euro (€) is Estonia's currency. The Estonian kroon (EEK) was replaced as the official currency when the Euro was introduced on January 1, 2011. Estonia joined the Eurozone, which is made up of countries in the European Union that use the Euro as their currency.

The symbol "€" denotes the Euro, which is divided into 100 cents. There are 1, 2, 5, 10, 20, and 50 cent coins, as well as 1 and 2 Euro coins, available for purchase. Banknotes are given in groups of 5, 10, 20, 50, 100, 200, and 500 Euros. Because Estonia and other countries in the Eurozone share a common currency, it is simpler for residents and tourists to transact within the country and across the Eurozone. In most Estonian cities and towns, there are ATMs that make it simple to get cash because the Euro is widely accepted there.

It is interesting to note that the Euro banknotes' design incorporates architectural elements from various periods of European history. Classical architecture can be seen on the 5 Euro note, Romanesque architecture can be seen on the 10 Euro note, Gothic architecture can be seen on the 20 Euro note, the Renaissance can be seen on the 50 Euro note, Baroque and Rococo architecture can be seen on the 100 Euro note, the Art Nouveau style can be seen on the 200 Euro note, and modern architecture can be seen on the 500 Euro note.

Useful Contacts in Estonia

The following Estonian contacts are helpful:

Estonia Embassy: Contact the Estonian Embassy in your country if you require assistance with visas, consular services, or any other official matter. They are able to offer you the necessary advice and information.

Services for Emergencies: Dial 112 in case of emergency. In Estonia, this is the one-stop emergency number, and depending on the situation, it will connect you to the police, ambulance, or fire departments.

Police in Estonia: In the event that you really want to report a non-crisis wrongdoing or look for general help from the police, you can contact the Estonian Police. They are able to provide details about the safety of the community as well as local laws and regulations. 110 is the most common police number.

Board of Customs and Taxes of Estonia: You can get in touch with the Estonian Tax and Customs Board if you have questions about taxation, customs, or import/export procedures. They are able to offer advice regarding customs regulations and tax issues. Additionally, their website provides online services and useful information.

Fund for Health Insurance: The Estonian Health Insurance Fund can be contacted with inquiries regarding healthcare services and health insurance coverage in Estonia. They are able to provide details about insurance policies, reimbursement procedures, and healthcare providers.

Information for Guests: The Estonian Tourist Information Center can be contacted if you are a tourist in Estonia and need information about local attractions, events, accommodations, or travel-related questions. You can get brochures, recommendations, and help planning your visit from them.

Board for Consumer Protection: The Estonian Consumer Protection Board can be contacted if you need assistance with disputes, unfair business practices, or consumer rights issues. They are able to offer guidance and information regarding regulations and laws pertaining to consumer protection.

Estonian Enterprise: Contact Enterprise Estonia if you are interested in investing, starting a business, or finding business opportunities in Estonia. Entrepreneurs, investors, and businesses seeking to operate in Estonia receive assistance and information from them.

Please keep in mind that these organizations' contact information may change over time, so if you need specific contact information, you should check the information on their official websites or in a local directory.

Chapter Five

Food

With its own distinct culinary heritage, Estonian cuisine incorporates influences from its neighbors, such as Russia, Latvia, and Finland. It is based on the rich traditions and history of the nation. Estonian cuisine is known for its natural, hearty, and straightforward flavors. It frequently makes use of regional ingredients like fish, meat, grains, and forest berries. The following are traditional Estonian dishes:

Leib: Dark bread: Black bread is a common ingredient in Estonian cuisine that has a significant cultural significance. Rye bread is flavorful and dense when baked in large, round loaves. Estonians frequently enjoy it with cheese, cold cuts, or fish on top and butter.

Mulgipuder: Mulgipuder, a traditional Estonian dish, can be found in the Mulgimaa region. Mashed potatoes are combined with barley or groats and served with pork or bacon. The creamy potatoes and filling grains make this a hearty and cozy meal.

Verivorst: Verivorst, also known as blood sausage, is a popular Christmas dish in Estonia. After being stuffed into natural casings made of blood, barley, and spices, it is typically cooked or fried. Verivorst is regularly joined by other bubbly dishes and lingonberry sauce.

Kama: Kama is a wonderful Estonian dessert that can be enjoyed as a bite or as a pastry. It is a finely ground mixture of roasted barley, rye, oat, and pea flour. Kama is typically combined with sour cream or buttermilk and sweetened with honey or sugar. It's very filling and has a nutty flavor.

The Baltic Herring, or Räim: In view of its situation along the Baltic Ocean, Estonia's cooking depends vigorously on fish. A popular fish in Estonia, Baltic herring is typically prepared by smoking or marinating. As a starter, onions, strong cream, or potatoes are frequently added.

Sauerkraut from Hapukapsas: Sauerkraut holds a special place in Estonian cuisine, particularly during the cooler months. It is made by fermenting finely shredded cabbage and salt, which results in a tart and slightly sour flavor. Sauerkraut is often added to traditional pies as a filling or as a side dish with meat dishes.

Cranberry kissel (Jhvikamoos): The forests of Estonia have a lot of cranberries, which are used in a lot of dishes. Cranberry kissel, a popular dessert, is made by cooking cranberries with water, sugar, and starch to thicken the mixture. Whip cream is typically added to it when it is chilled.

These are just a few of the many unique and delectable dishes Estonia has to offer. By exploring the country's cuisine, you can discover a delightful combination of traditional flavors and ingredients that are a reflection of the country's distinct cultural heritage.

Drinks

The drinking culture in Estonia, a beautiful country in Northern Europe, is diverse and rich. Estonians are proud of their alcoholic and non-alcoholic beverages, which are influenced by their history, customs, and regional ingredients. Let's look at some of Estonia's most popular drinks.

Vana Estonia: This is the most well-known liqueur from Estonia, and it is often called the "national drink." Vana Tallinn is a dark liqueur made with rum and spices like cinnamon, vanilla, citrus oils, and rum extracts. It is typically consumed neat or in cocktails and has a distinct and robust flavor. The name of the liqueur, which means "Old Tallinn," is a nod to Estonia's capital city.

Craft Beers from Saaremaa: In recent years, the craft beer scene in Estonia has grown, and Saaremaa, Estonia's largest island, is known for its excellent breweries. The island brags an assortment of specialty brews, including beers, ales, stouts, and IPAs. Pöide Brewery, Leisi Brewery, and Kuressaare Brewery are three well-known breweries in Saaremaa. These beers often have a unique Estonian flavor because they use local ingredients like wildflowers or juniper berries.

Kali: In Estonia, kali is a traditional fermented, non-alcoholic beverage. Dark rye bread and water undergo fermentation to make it. Kali is frequently compared to a light, non-alcoholic beer because of its tangy flavor. It can be found in most Estonian supermarkets and traditional taverns, making it a popular summer drink.

Vodka: Viru Valge: Viru Valge is a well-known Estonian vodka brand, and vodka holds a special place in Estonian drinking culture. It is made from grains of high quality and is distilled multiple times, giving it a smooth and clean taste. Viru Valge Vodka is typically consumed neat, on the rocks, or as the foundation for a variety of cocktails.

Estonian bourbons: There is a thriving cider industry in Estonia, which produces a variety of delicious ciders made from apples grown locally. These ciders come in a variety of flavors, including traditional dry and crisp varieties as well as sweeter varieties that are flavored with berries or herbs. Siidrikoda, Jaanihanso, and Nudist Ciders are among the well-known brands of Estonian cider.

Sap of birch: Estonians use the birch sap, known as "kasemahl," in the spring, when the trees emerge from winter. Birch sap is highly prized for its health benefits and is a refreshing, clear, slightly sweet beverage. It can be enjoyed on its own or as part of desserts and cocktails.

Kvass: Kvass is a traditional fermented beverage that is popular in Estonia as well as Russia. Black or rye bread is fermented with water, sugar, and occasionally fruits or herbs to make it. Kvass is a popular summertime beverage because of its tart, slightly sour flavor.

These are just a few of the many delicious beverages available in Estonia. Estonia has a diverse and vibrant drinking culture that reflects its history and distinctive flavors, and you can sample traditional liqueurs, craft beers, and non-alcoholic specialties here.

Eating Out in Estonia

With a blend of international influences and traditional Estonian cuisine, dining out in Estonia is a delightful culinary experience. The country has a thriving food scene, with a wide range of cafes, restaurants, and other establishments to suit a wide range of preferences. Estonia has something to please everyone's palate, whether you prefer regional cuisine or international flavors.

The simplicity of traditional Estonian cuisine and its reliance on locally sourced ingredients define it. "Kama," a mixture of roasted barley, rye, oat, and pea flour, is one of the most well-known traditional dishes. It is typically served with buttermilk or kefir. It has a distinctive texture and flavor that should be tried.

The hearty dishes known as "seapraad" (roast pork) and "hakklihapallid" (meatballs) can be found in Estonian cuisine. Sauerkraut, potatoes, and lingonberry jam are all delicious sides that go well with these dishes. Additionally, fish dishes are popular, with salmon and Baltic herring appearing frequently.

There are a lot of restaurants in Estonia that serve a variety of international cuisines. You can explore a variety of options, including Italian, French, Asian, Mediterranean, and more, in larger cities like Tallinn. Particularly in the capital city, there are numerous restaurants of high quality that have received international recognition.

Estonia's Old Town, a UNESCO World Heritage Site, is an excellent starting point for your culinary explorations. Charming cafes and restaurants serving Estonian and international cuisine line its cobblestone streets. While taking in the medieval setting, you can savor traditional Estonian fare here.

You can get a taste of contemporary Estonian cuisine by dining in modern establishments that combine local ingredients with cutting-edge cooking methods. Many of these establishments place an emphasis on using organic, seasonal, and fresh produce from nearby farms. They frequently offer tasting menus that showcase the talents of talented chefs and highlight the variety of Estonian flavors.

Estonia has a thriving cafe culture if you prefer dining more casually. There are cozy cafes all over the country that serve light meals, homemade pastries, and freshly brewed coffee. This is a fantastic opportunity to socialize with the locals, unwind, and take in the laid-back vibe.

In recent years, Estonia has become increasingly accommodating to individuals with dietary preferences or restrictions. Vegetarian, vegan, and gluten-free options are now available at a lot of restaurants. If you tell the staff about your specific dietary requirements, they will almost always be happy to accommodate you.

Depending on the establishment and the location, the cost of dining out in Estonia can range from affordable to expensive. In general, dining out is more affordable in rural and smaller towns, whereas upscale restaurants in larger cities may charge more. Check the menu and prices before you go or ask locals for suggestions that are within your budget.

All in all, eating out in Estonia gives a magnificent chance to relish conventional Estonian dishes, as well as investigate worldwide flavors. Estonia's culinary scene is diverse and exciting, with traditional eateries serving hearty local fare and contemporary establishments pushing the boundaries of gastronomy. You'll be satisfied and want to go back for more.

Estonians Traditional Habits

The traditional practices and customs of Estonia, a small Baltic nation in Northern Europe, are a reflection of its rich cultural heritage. The following are important aspects of Estonian customs:

Life in the sauna: Saunas are deeply ingrained in Estonian customs and hold a special place in their culture. Saunas are regarded as places of spiritual and physical purification. Saunas are regarded as a means of unwinding, socializing, and enhancing one's overall health by Estonians who believe in their therapeutic properties. Families and friends frequently congregate in the sauna to take a steam bath, converse, and even perform traditional sauna rituals like whisking each other with birch branches.

Folklore and song: Estonian folklore and choral singing have a significant impact on the country's cultural identity. The grand "Laulupidu" singing festivals are grand gatherings of thousands of singers to perform traditional Estonian songs. UNESCO has designated these celebrations as intangible cultural heritage because they have been observed since the 19th century. Estonians take great pride in their choral tradition, which is why schools teach singing and folk dances to keep these traditions alive.

Connection to Nature: Estonians have a strong connection to their natural surroundings and a profound appreciation for nature. This is because of Estonia's numerous lakes and rivers, picturesque landscapes, and lush forests. Fishing, berry picking, and spending time in the great outdoors are all part of traditional practices. Additionally, many Estonians own summer cottages in rural areas, where they spend weekends and holidays to relax and take in the natural beauty.

Coats of Arms: The "rahvariided," or traditional Estonian clothing, is unique to each region of the country. Embroidery, vibrant colors, and intricate patterns adorn these folk costumes. They are frequently donned on special occasions like weddings, folk festivals, and national celebrations. Estonians take great pride in preserving and displaying their customary attire, which is a representation of their cultural heritage and a sign of their identity as a nation.

Cuisine from the past: Simple, hearty, and sourced locally, Estonian traditional cuisine is characterized by these characteristics. Potatoes, pork, fish, rye bread, and dairy products are staples. The "mulgipuder," which is mashed potatoes with pork and groats, the "kama," which is a mixture of roasted grains, the "kiluvileib," which is a sandwich with sprats, and various desserts that are based on berries, are examples of traditional dishes. These dishes are a reflection of Estonia's agricultural roots and the seasonal availability of its ingredients.

Celebrations in the Summer: In Estonia, Midsummer's Eve, also known as "Jaanipäev" or "Jaanihtu," is one of the most significant traditional holidays. It commemorates the summer solstice and is associated with ancient pagan practices. It is observed on June 23. People from Estonia gather around bonfires to sing and dance, eat and drink traditional foods, and participate in a variety of outdoor activities.

Midsummer's Eve is a time to bond with others and celebrate nature's beauty.

These ancient customs are deeply ingrained in Estonian culture, where they are still cherished and handed down from generation to generation. They are crucial to the preservation of Estonia's history and the development of a strong sense of national identity among Estonians

Shopping and Nightlife in Estonia

Estonia, a vibrant Baltic nation in Northern Europe, has an exciting nightlife scene and a unique combination of modern shopping experiences. Estonia has something for everyone, from fashion to local crafts to a lively night out. Let's take a look at Estonia's nightlife and shopping:

Estonian shopping:

Tallinn: Tallinn, Estonia's capital, is a shopping mecca. Shops, gift shops, and art galleries abound in the charming Old Town, a UNESCO World Heritage Site. Traditional Estonian handicrafts, such as hand-knitted woolens, ceramics, and wooden items, can be found here. Popular shopping centers like Viru Keskus and Solaris have a mix of local and international brands.

Quarter for Rotermann: The Rotermann Quarter is a trendy shopping destination near Tallinn's Old Town. Modern boutiques, design stores, and concept shops now occupy this redeveloped industrial area. Here, you can find a wide range of products for fashion, design, and home decor.

Tartu: Tartu, the second-largest city in Estonia, is well-known for its youthful and energetic atmosphere. Tartu Kaubamaja, a huge department store with a wide range of products, is the center of the main shopping area. Additionally, the city is home to numerous second-hand stores, antique shops, and smaller boutiques.

Pärnu: Pärnu is where you should go if you want to shop along the coast. It has beautiful beaches with sand and a lively promenade with shops and boutiques. Everything from local handicrafts to fashion and accessories can be found here.

In Estonia, the nightlife:

Tallinn: Tallinn's nightlife is well-known for its vibrancy and variety. There are a lot of bars, clubs, and lounges in the city that cater to different tastes. Bar hopping is a popular activity in the Old Town, where you can find cozy pubs, cocktail bars, and venues for live music. The Telliskivi and Kalamaja neighborhoods are well-known for their hip bars and unconventional venues.

Tartu: Tartu has a thriving nightlife scene because it is a university town. Numerous bars, clubs, and pubs in the city cater to a lively, young crowd. Popular areas like Raekoja Plats (Town Hall Square) and Ülikooli Street have a lot of nightlife establishments.

Pärnu: During the summer, when tourists flock to the resort town, Pärnu's nightlife comes to life. You can dance the night away at beach clubs, nightclubs, and open-air venues. Reputable DJs and musicians also attend the Pärnu Beach Festival, which is a huge success.

Other towns: Viljandi, Kuressaare, and Haapsalu, three other cities in Estonia, each have their own distinct nightlife scenes. With cozy pubs, live music performances, and cultural events, these cities provide a more relaxed and intimate setting.

When planning your trip to Estonia, it is recommended to check local listings, websites, and recommendations for up-to-date information due to the fact that nightlife and shopping scenes can change over time.

Chapter Six

Language in Estonia

The rich linguistic landscape of Estonia, a small nation in Northern Europe, reflects its history and cultural diversity. Estonian, a Finno-Ugric language that is both closely related to Finnish and distantly related to Hungarian, is the country's official language. Let's investigate the characteristics of Estonian and the country's linguistic context.

Estonian is spoken:

The Estonian language is spoken by the majority of the population and is the native tongue of the Estonian people. It is well-known for its distinctive phonetic characteristics, such as the presence of vowel harmony, which requires that all vowels in a word fall into the same category—front or back. Diphthongs, which are combinations of two vowels within a syllable, are also prevalent in the language.

Since Estonian is an agglutinative language, suffixes are used to express grammatical relationships with the root word. This element considers the arrangement of long and complex words. "To the local one's," for instance, is the meaning of the word "omamaisele."

Languages of Minority:

Estonian is one of several minority languages spoken there. Russian, which is primarily spoken by the ethnic Russian community that immigrated to Estonia during the Soviet era, is one notable minority language. Russian is still very popular among older generations and in some urban areas.

Ukrainian, Belarusian, and Finnish are among the other minority languages spoken in Estonia. The country's smaller communities speak these languages.

Language Education and Policy:

In accordance with the linguistic rights of minority communities, Estonia has implemented policies to support and safeguard the Estonian language. The country has focused on promoting the use of Estonian in various spheres of society ever since it regained independence in 1991.

Although some schools that cater to specific language communities may offer education in their respective languages, Estonian is the primary language of instruction in schools. Additionally, to assist non-native speakers in integrating into society and learning the language, the Estonian government offers language support programs.

Technology in Language:

Additionally, Estonia has embraced digital advancements and developed a reputation for putting a strong emphasis on technology. The use and growth of the Estonian language are greatly aided by language technology. Spell-checkers, language corpora, and online language resources are just a few of the language technology initiatives that aid in language usage and preservation.

Proficiency in Multiple Languages and Linguistics:

Estonia has placed a greater emphasis on multilingualism in recent years. English is widely spoken and taught as a first language in schools, particularly among younger generations. German, French, and Spanish are among the other foreign languages that are frequently studied.

In general, Estonia is a society with multiple languages, but Estonian is the country's primary language. Respecting the linguistic diversity of its minority communities, the nation has taken steps to preserve and promote the Estonian language. Estonia's history, culture, and position as a modern, technologically advanced nation are all reflected in this linguistic richness.

Greetings in Estonia

The culture and traditions of Estonia are reflected in the way people greet one another in social situations. The way people greet each other is influenced by the Estonian language, which is the country's primary language. The following are some Estonian greetings and customs:

Tere: In Estonian, the simplest and most common greeting is "Tere." It very well may be utilized in any circumstance, whether formal or casual, and is proper for all ages.

Tere hommikust, which means "good morning," is used only in the early morning until about noon. Greeting someone at the beginning of the day in this manner is courteous.

Tere päevast - Similar to "tere päevast," "tere päevast" is used to greet someone during the day, between noon and early evening. It means "good day" in English.

Tere õhtust - When the sun starts to set, Estonians use "tere õhtust" to say "goodbye." From late in the afternoon until late at night, it is an appropriate greeting.

Nägemist is an Estonian word that means "goodbye" and is used to say goodbye. It is a courteous way to say goodbye to someone or end a conversation.

Tere tulemast - The greeting "Tere tulemast" is commonly used to welcome guests or visitors. It is a welcoming and friendly way to welcome someone.

What is it? - "Kuidas läheb?" is a common question among Estonians. to inquire about a person's health. It means "How are you doing?" and is a common way to greet friends, coworkers, and strangers.

Head päeva and head htut mean, respectively, "have a good day" and "have a good evening." They are commonly used to congratulate someone on their day or evening.

These expressions, "have a nice continuation of the day" and "have a nice continuation of the evening," respectively, are referred to as "kena päeva jätku" and "kena htut jätku." They are frequently used to say goodbye to someone or to wish them a happy day or evening.

In Estonia, it is customary to shake hands when meeting someone, especially in formal settings, in addition to verbal greetings. A hug or a kiss on the cheek may be exchanged as a form of greeting for friends and family.

The Estonian culture, which places a high value on politeness and warmth in social interactions, is reflected in the general manner in which Estonians greet one another.

Custom and Laws in Estonia

Estonia is a nation in Northern Europe that is well-known for its cutting-edge digital infrastructure and e-governance programs. Estonia adheres to a legal framework that promotes transparency, efficiency, and respect for individual rights when it comes to customs and laws. An overview of Estonia's laws and customs is as follows: you

Constitution: The Estonian Constitution, which was enacted in 1992, is the country's most important law. Freedom of speech, equality before the law, and the right to life, liberty, and security are just a few of the fundamental freedoms it upholds.

Legal Structure: The civil law system in Estonia is influenced by Germanic and Scandinavian legal systems. Written laws and statutes form the foundation of the legal system, and the judiciary is crucial in interpreting and applying the law.

Legitimate Codes: The majority of Estonian laws are codified into various legal codes. The Constitution, the Penal Code, the Civil Code, the Administrative Procedure Code, the Criminal Procedure Code, and the Commercial Code are a few of the most significant codes.

E-Governance: Estonia's digital governance system is well-known. Numerous e-services are available to citizens, such as e-voting, e-tax filing, and e-residency. The digital infrastructure's goals are to make bureaucratic procedures easier to follow and increase transparency.

Individual Liberty and Human Rights: Personal liberty and human rights are fundamental principles in Estonia. The country respects the right to a fair trial, freedom of thought, conscience, and religion, and the prohibition of torture and inhuman treatment and is a signatory to a number of international human rights conventions, including the European Convention on Human Rights.

Nondiscrimination and equality: Estonia promotes nondiscrimination and equality. The Constitution enshrined the principle of equal treatment, and there is legislation to combat discrimination based on race, gender, nationality, disability, and other factors.

Family Law: In Estonia, marriage, divorce, child custody, and adoption are all governed by family law. Civil marriages and registered partnerships between same-sex couples are both recognized by the law.

Commercial and Business Law: Estonia is known for its ease of doing business and business-friendly regulations. Businesses, contracts, intellectual property rights, and other commercial matters are governed by the Commercial Code.

Environmental safeguarding: Estonia has environmental protection and sustainable development laws in place. Environmental impact assessments, waste management, nature conservation, and air and water quality are all governed by laws.

Rights in Intellectual Property: Copyrights, trademarks, patents, and other intellectual property assets are safeguarded by laws in Estonia, which uphold intellectual property rights.

It is essential to keep in mind that laws are subject to change, so the most up-to-date and accurate information regarding Estonian customs and laws should be obtained from official sources or from legal professionals.

Chapter Seven

Travel Tips

Here are some movement ways to visit Estonia:

Climate and Seasons: Estonia has a calm environment, with gentle summers and cold winters. Pack appropriately, with hotter attire assuming you're visiting during the colder months. Really take a look at the weather conditions conjecture before your outing to be ready.

Visa Prerequisites: Check in the event that you require a visa to enter Estonia in light of your ethnicity. Numerous nations have without visa admittance to Estonia for as long as 90 days inside a six-month time span. Guarantee your visa is legitimate for no less than a half year past your arranged takeoff date.

Money: The authority cash of Estonia is the Euro (EUR). Make a point to have some money close by for more modest foundations, as Mastercards are not generally acknowledged all over.

Language: The authority language is Estonian, however English is generally spoken, particularly in vacationer regions and significant urban communities. You shouldn't have huge correspondence issues, yet learning a couple of essential Estonian phrases is dependably useful.

Transportation: Estonia has a proficient public transportation framework. Tallinn, the capital city, has a very much associated organization of transports, cable cars, and trolleybuses. Consider buying an electronic vehicle card for accommodation. Taxis are likewise accessible, yet try to utilize authorized taxicabs or ride-sharing administrations.

Wellbeing: Estonia is by and large a protected nation, however it's dependably really smart to play it safe. Watch out for your things, particularly in packed regions, and be mindful of pickpockets. Having travel protection that covers health related crises and outing cancellation is prudent.

Web Access: Estonia is known for its phenomenal web framework. Most inns, cafés, and bistros offer free Wi-Fi. On the off chance that you want consistent web access, consider buying a neighborhood SIM card or compact Wi-Fi gadget.

Social Decorum: Estonians are for the most part amiable and held. It's standard to welcome individuals with a strong handshake and keep in touch. Take off your shoes while entering somebody's home, and follow essential social graces while eating out.

Must-Visit Spots: Investigate Tallinn's charming Old Town, an UNESCO World Legacy Site, with its middle age engineering and cobblestone roads. Visit Lahemaa Public Park for its wonderful nature trails and various untamed life. Tartu, Estonia's second-biggest city, is known for its energetic understudy culture and noteworthy college.

Neighborhood Cooking: Test customary Estonian dishes like dark bread, sauerkraut, smoked fish, and good stews. Try not to pass up attempting the neighborhood alcohol, Vana Tallinn, and the well known sweet treat, kama.

Nature and Outside Exercises: Estonia flaunts delightful woods, lakes, and shoreline. Investigate the Lahemaa Public Park, Soomaa Public Park, or go island jumping to Saaremaa or Hiiumaa. Appreciate climbing, paddling, cycling, or bird-watching in the peaceful regular environmental elements.

Make sure to actually look at the most recent tourism warnings and rules before your outing, as conditions and guidelines might change. Partake in your visit to Estonia!

Do's and Don'ts For Tourist in Estonia

When visiting or interacting with Estonians, be mindful of the following guidelines:

Do's:

Always shake hands strongly and maintain eye contact when greeting others. Directness and a polite greeting are valued by Estonians.

Be mindful of one's own space. Estonians typically value privacy to a certain extent, but they may object to excessive physical contact or invasions of personal space.

Be on time for all meetings and appointments. People in Estonia value punctuality and expect others to be prompt.

When entering someone's home, unless otherwise instructed, remove your shoes. In Estonia, removing shoes at the door is common practice.

Try to pick up a few basic Estonian words and phrases. Even though many Estonians speak English, it is appreciated to try to communicate in their language.

Do adhere to the regulations. Respecting local regulations and customs is essential because Estonia is renowned for its strict adherence to them.

Do take pleasure in Estonia's natural splendor. Take the time to look around and take in the beauty of the country's forests, lakes, and stunning landscapes.

Don'ts:

In public settings, do not speak loudly or interrupt. In general, Estonians value a quieter and more reserved demeanor in public.

Avoid being too familiar or too expressive. Estonians are typically reserved and may feel uneasy around people who show too much emotion or are familiar with them.

Don't say anything negative about the country or its past. People in Estonia are proud of their heritage and may find insulting remarks or insensitive jokes offensive.

Try not to litter or harm the climate. Littering is considered disrespectful in Estonia, which has a strong commitment to environmental preservation.

Don't assume that everyone speaks Russian well. Even though most people speak Russian, not everyone is fluent, so it's best to find out what language they prefer before starting a conversation.

Unless the other person initiates the conversation, do not discuss political issues or the Soviet past. Some Estonians may find these subjects to be sensitive, so it's best to be cautious and respect their boundaries.

Sauna manners should not be ignored. If you're invited to a sauna in Estonia, it's important to know how to behave, like sitting on a towel and following the host's instructions. Keep in mind that these are only general guidelines; individual preferences may differ. You'll probably have a good time in Estonia if you treat people with respect, keep an open mind, and pay attention to the culture.

Religion and Beliefs

Throughout its history, Estonia's religion and beliefs have undergone significant transformations due to a variety of influences, including political shifts, cultural advancements, and external influences. Estonia's religious diversity and relatively high levels of secularism are now well-known.

The Estonian mythology, also known as the Estonian native faith or Maausk, was the indigenous religion in Estonia's predominantly pagan past. The worship of nature, ancestors, and deities associated with natural elements were central to this ancient belief system. However, Estonia gradually converted to Christianity beginning in the 13th century, primarily under the influence of the Teutonic Knights and the Livonian Order.

Estonia underwent religious transformations during the 16th-century Reformation as Lutheran Protestantism gained prominence. Estonian culture and society were forever altered as a result of Lutheranism's rise to prominence as the dominant Christian denomination. Even though its influence has waned over time, Lutheranism is still the largest Christian denomination in Estonia today.

In the 19th century, Estonia experienced a flurry of spiritual and religious movements, including the spread of Methodism and other Protestant denominations as well as the spread of Orthodox Christianity. Particularly in northeastern Estonia, the Russian Orthodox Church developed a significant following among the Russian-speaking population. The Estonian-speaking population has adherents to Methodism and other Protestant movements.

Due to political shifts and two world wars, the 20th century in Estonia saw tumultuous times for religion. The Estonian Soviet Socialist Republic suppressed religious practices and implemented an atheistic ideology from 1944 to 1991. Restrictions were imposed on religious institutions and churches, and religious adherents frequently faced discrimination. As a result, many Estonians lost faith in organized religion and became less religious.

Religious pluralism has resurfaced in Estonia since it regained its independence in 1991, and religious freedom has been protected by law. Today, the religious landscape in Estonia is distinguished by its diversity and notable secularism. The number of self-identified Lutherans has decreased, despite the fact that

Lutheranism continues to be the most popular religious group. Numerous Pentecostal and charismatic movements, the Russian Orthodox Church, Baptist congregations, and other Christian denominations have gained followers.

Additionally, the emergence of neopagan and New Age movements is a recent development in Estonia. People who want to reconnect with the country's pre-Christian roots and nature-based spirituality are becoming more and more interested in the revival of the native faith of Estonia (Maausk). Among Estonians, new age spiritual practices like meditation, yoga, and mindfulness have also gained popularity.

A significant portion of the Estonian population identifies as non-religious or atheist, in addition to Christianity and other alternative faiths. In Europe, Estonia has one of the highest rates of secularism and atheism. A secular worldview, which places an emphasis on rationality and science over traditional religious teachings, is embraced by many Estonians.

In general, Estonian religion and beliefs are a reflection of a diverse web of social, cultural, and historical influences. Traditional Christian denominations, alternative spiritualities, and a predominant secular mindset make up the country's evolving religious landscape. In Estonian society, the right to practice one's beliefs or not practice any religion at all is respected and protected.

Conclusion

In conclusion, Estonia provides a travel experience that is truly original and captivating. This tiny Baltic nation is an unforgettable destination because it seamlessly combines its stunning natural beauty, vibrant modern culture, and rich history. Estonia has something for every kind of traveler, from the medieval streets of Tallinn's Old Town to the peaceful forests of Lahemaa National Park.

All through this movement guide, we have investigated Estonia's different attractions and featured its surprising milestones. A glimpse into Estonia's past is provided by the enchanting beauty of its architecture, such as the Alexander Nevsky Cathedral and Toompea Castle. Meanwhile, the country's vibrant present is showcased by the thriving cultural scene, which includes contemporary art galleries and music festivals.

Another highlight is Estonia's unspoiled landscapes, which include vast forests, picturesque lakes, and captivating coastal areas. Nature lovers can take in the tranquil surroundings of Soomaa National Park or Saaremaa Island's singular beauty. Additionally, Estonia's dedication to environmental sustainability and digital innovation further enhances the travel experience, making it an environmentally conscious and forward-thinking destination.

Additionally, the welcoming and friendly locals of Estonia add to the country's overall charm. Every interaction reveals their pride in their heritage, customs, and language, offering travelers an authentic and immersive experience.

Estonia has it all, whether you're looking for a new adventure, history, culture, or nature. The goal of this travel guide is to show you the amazing things the country has to offer and help you find its many attractions. You will be captivated by Estonia's beauty, inspired by its history, and welcomed by its people from the moment you arrive to the moment you depart.

In conclusion, Estonia is a treasure trove in Northern Europe that is just waiting to be discovered and appreciated. Therefore, pack your bags, become engrossed in the magic of Estonia, and set out on an unforgettable journey that will provide you with memories that will last a lifetime.

Printed in Great Britain
by Amazon

30783721R00071